he's *so* MASC

CHRIS TSE ———————————— he's *so* MASC

*For Amy
with very best wishes.
Ngā mihi
Chris*

AUCKLAND
UNIVERSITY
PRESS

This book is for Leight

First published 2018
Auckland University Press
University of Auckland
Private Bag 92019
Auckland 1142
New Zealand
www.press.auckland.ac.nz

ISBN 978 1 86940 887 9

Published with the assistance of Creative New Zealand

ARTS COUNCIL OF NEW ZEALAND TOI AOTEAROA

A catalogue record for this book is available from the National Library of New Zealand

Book design by Katrina Duncan
Cover design by Greg Simpson

This book was printed on FSC® certified paper

Printed by 1010 Printing International Ltd

Contents

'I have lost my origin
 and I don't want to find it again'.
— Björk

'All the world is all I am'.
— Tori Amos

'I want to fit—I've got to get man-sized'.
— PJ Harvey

Intro

Shut the fuck up.

Can you hear that?

Listen.

Wolves!

Wolves with roses in their teeth.
Roses with blood dripping
from their petals. Petals skimming
across a ballroom floor in an '80s music video.

Lightning crashes—their bright eyes
lock on—very, very frightening indeed.

The wolves are closing in
on the ballroom while the band members
look out and brace themselves
for the conflict to come. Shit just got real.
They pick up their instruments
and clear their throats.

1 and 2 and 3 and—

Belated backstory

There were animals. They came to me
with their bloodstained murmurs

choking the night, the weight of misery
a gloom in their throats. Beasts of all

shapes and mythologies scratching
at the soil around my grave, each one

driven by its own unique hunger
but all intent on writing my end.

I can almost run my fingers through
the sun-streaked strands of those days

when I was nothing but a silhouette
disappearing into fog—just a sketch.

I could step into a crowd and never
resurface. No one would suspect a thing.

Heavy lifting

Once, I climbed a tree
too tall for climbing
and threw my voice out
into the world. I screamed.
I hollered. I snapped
innocent branches. I took the view
as a vivid but painful truth gifted
to me, but did not think to lay down
my own sight in recompense.
All I wanted was someone to say
they could hear me, but the tree said
that in order to be heard I must
first let silence do the heavy lifting
and clear my mind of any
questions and anxieties
such as contemplating whether
I am the favourite son. If I am not,
I am open to being a favourite uncle
or an ex-lover whose hands still cover
the former half's eyes. I'll probably never
have children of my own to disappoint
so I'll settle for being famous instead
with my mouth forced open on TV like
a Venus fly-trap lip-synching for its life.
The first and the last of everything
are always connected by
the dotted line of choice.
If there is an order to such things,
then surely I should resist it.

Punctum

This is my blood oath with myself: the only
dead Chinese person I'll write about from now on
is me.   I know   I know

it'll do me no good   to drag my body
through the town square
to prove that it wasn't me

who set fire to the school to avoid my maths exam
who shot the prince in the bushes behind the barn
where the queers get together to   talk

nor was it me
who leaked those emails about which All Black
the Prime Minister would bottom for.   But

I hope my name and track record with   unsolved crimes
will finally be cleared so I can get on with my new life
as a Chinese girl

behind the counter being bullied into saying 'fried rice'
by the *gwai lo* in the cheap suit. In between scoops
of sweet and sour pork   I curse the heavens

for saddling me with a mediocre work ethic
which has kept me here for five years despite knowing
there is no career progression   unless I

marry my boss's son, who is studying to be
a capitalist like all good Chinese boys. He's got a small dick
and no sense of rhythm   but our children

will likely be pleasant-looking enough
to be background extras   in a re-enactment
of Helen Clark's apology for the poll tax—that is,

if their father allows them to have the arts in their lives.
I'll be their proud stage mother and encourage them
to audition for awards-bait roles—for example,

the unapologetic sex addict still burying porn
in his parents' backyard

the pregnant teen goth who must decide whether to keep
her subscription to Evanescence's monthly fan club newsletter

the paraplegic hooker with a heart of gold
made from melted-down Oscars

the proud gay man pretending to be straight
to be made partner at his father's law firm in 1940s Austria

the racist spiritual healer about to inherit
a hand sanitiser empire in Birmingham, Alabama.

But in all likelihood my children will have only
moderately humble acting careers playing
accountants, taxi drivers and restaurateurs

to supplement their primary incomes as
accountants, taxi drivers and restaurateurs.
I'll go to my next grave   wondering

whether I pushed them hard enough to never settle
for being the token Asian in a crowd scene or
the Asian acquaintance in an ethnically diverse television series

set in New York City, who is only mentioned and never seen
unless you pause at 12.29 of season 4 episode 6
and carefully inspect the photographs on the wall—

there, that's my youngest standing in the back row
of a wedding group shot.   Can you see her?
                Can you see her?

Tonight, Matthew

Thirty-something and—*shit!*—

Windows is shutting down—

again with the lag and tidings.

If I don't have a name for it, how do I recover?

Maybe I should push more.

But then I see the riverbank

sluiced in red from the sacrificial high season.

I can't get on board with that, no siree!

Artistic men standing by with their motivations and fashionable

facial hair.   Me? I prefer an 'I grew up like this' aesthetic

for my unsuccessful auditions.

Thirty-something and—

what's that crash scene up over the horizon?

When I grow up, I'll impress the world

with how calmly I can walk away

from exploding cars/buildings/spaceships.

My life story will fill pages of

Google search results—instant proof

I'll neither confirm nor deny

when the time comes to sell out.

Instead, I suggest you hunt through

second-hand stores looking for

my obscure inspirations and give new life

to *Goosebumps*® reading lights.

I'm going to

fuck it up.   (Don't   fuck it up.)

I guess I'll sit here silently

in the name of art until someone dares

to tell me it's my fault

they know too much about me.

Has someone written a book about that?

Thirty-something and

Ivy adding class to ambition, where the walls

are fit for purpose, but the sky is not.

Tonight, Matthew, I'm going to

disappear into the dark side

of the stage.   Tonight, I'll just watch.

Chris Tse and His Imaginary Band

We were brighter when the world didn't know
about us or our rock 'n' roll dreams. Now
we dress in black, but we're not depressed—
we're just backlit, per record label instructions.
Fans come and go, but true fans stick with you
through the stigma of rib removal and that feud
with Jem and the Holograms. Nobody can win.
Nowadays, the world is made of oysters and
everyone's had a taste. Can I just say that I think
I've done too many drugs. (Or maybe it's gout?)
The bloggers won't stop reading into our
matching tattoos. Yes, they're of each other's wives,
but what's that got to do with the music?
Everyone has forgotten we're an imaginary band.
A suggested path back to relevancy: nip slip—rehab
ten-trip—a greatest hits. It'll take an untimely death
to seal our legend. No veins for overdose,
no doomed flight. Buried by a mountain
of french fries—that's how I want us all to go.

Artist's impression of the poet is not drawn to scale

This is the poet behind the mask
    of a matinée idol
who has no emergency contact
and whose love songs are built
with gender-neutral pronouns.

Many are surprised that the poet is shorter
in real life, yet is still as susceptible
to mythology as the rest of us.

  ~

There are points
in the poet's life that cannot be accurately
rendered by any artist
or the poet himself.

Well, you're obviously a crap painter,
said the art teacher to the poet.

What stress, if any, to place
on the young poet's arm
caught in a clothing recycling bin
or his hand thrown
through the glass of his front door?

  ~

This is the poet masquerading
   as a rock star
   as a local celebrity

and in this piece:
       as a rugby player
       as a straight man
cutting through the pack
to score the winning try
while the crowd cheers
       PO-ET! PO-ET!

He doesn't bother looking out
towards the stands for that special someone
or something.
       The mud caking his face
gives way to tear tracks and a flash of guilt:
to play this championship game
he left a poem to walk home alone.
This is the poet as neglectful father.

Like a queen

I should be king
I should be torn from your stuffy pages

                              I should be monster
          I should be undeterred by scars on shoulder blades

I should be tempted
I should be blackened, cum-stained and bleeding from love

                         I should be everything
            I should be twenty-something with no heel

I should be wanton
I should be leaning over ledges with my fortune

                             I should be happy
              I should be a bottle that never empties

I should be cruel
I should be crime scene bathed in unforgiving flash

                             I should be looking
       I should be Maria on a hilltop desperate for reception

I should be mirrored
I should be blanketed in folds of rolling silk

                               I should be child
            I should be tender at their protests

I should be ready
I should be volume up on open roads

I should be paper
I should be leading you all into war

I should be visible
I should be on every street corner as is

I should be bold
I should be the reason you know my name

I should be spill
I should be more than enough

I should be queen
I should be your closing credits

I was a self-loathing poet

There's an app that lets you see other poets in your vicinity. Some of these poets are 'non-scene' and promise discretion (they usually have headless author photos, or blurry, suggestive close-ups of their pens), while others proudly state that they are published and gladly share their literary CV. Some even write non-fiction! There are those who will chat only if you've published a minimum of eight poems, whereas others are open to accommodating poetry-curious prose writers. The profiles that state 'I'm not racist, but no haikus' really irk me and leave me feeling inadequate. Once, the app said there was a poet about five metres away from me. I didn't instigate a chat session, but I'm sure I heard faint tapping coming from the other side of my bedroom wall.

~

I spy poets in the streets—some of them I recognise from the app. They clutch their open Moleskines, pens poised with an air of intent: *I am capturing this moment*. Their choice of writing instrument is a code, signalling formal preferences (for example, biros for free verse; fountain pens for sonnets; blood-tipped quills for responses to dead white male poets). Sometimes our eyes will catch and we exchange a loaded look before pulling away. Although seeing another poet in the flesh—sharing that illicit gaze—moves me to recognise I'm not alone, I'm simultaneously repulsed. And yet I will spend many hours after these encounters aggressively dissecting those shy, flirty holds. As a young man this wreaks havoc on my journey to self-discovery. Why can't I write prose like everybody else? Will I ever afford avocado on toast? How am I so different?

~

A few years ago I became involved with another poet. He was a friend of a friend who asked for my number after spotting me loitering at the back of a book launch. He'd been published in *Deep Odes* and *Pun Ghazellers* and had strong views about publishing equality for poets. We spent hours sharing lines from our favourite collections and he impressed me with gossip about acclaimed novelists who were secretly writing poems on the down-low. About two weeks after we met he wrote a sonnet about me. My first instinct was to bolt, but I didn't, telling myself to stick with what was promising to be a good thing. Besides, the sonnet was really quite lovely and no one had ever shown such an interest in my writing before. Then he started talking about finding a writing studio together and introducing me to his writing group. I went into panic mode again. He said I needed to tell my parents I was a poet. (I was pretty sure my mother already suspected, as mothers tend to. She would ask me whether I was reading any good novels and I would respond with something vague, like, 'I don't have time to read novels at the moment'.) It turns out this was the make-or-break, so I cut all contact with him. I simply stopped calling him, and he gave up attempting to reach me after a week. I'm not proud of how I called it off. Perhaps if I had been braver back then—ready to admit to myself that I was a poet—things might be different now.

~

Older poets take a liking to me, but I politely decline their advances. One invited me to accompany him on a trip to a literary festival in Sydney, which was tempting (a free trip to Sydney!), but I suspected he wanted something in return like feedback on the third draft of his new collection or someone to create a master index of his first lines. Many of these poets assume that all young Asian poets want an older European poet to shower them with attention and constructive criticism. I've had enough of these encounters to realise that many of them are in shaky relationships with their publishers and never got the chance to experiment with poetry in their youth. It's hard to explain to them that their persistence, at first flattering, creeps me out. 'Know your niche', a poet friend says to me, 'and play the field that way'. But I just want to find a poet my age, preferably one open to using unconventional line breaks. I've come to realise that the poets I lust after in my head tend to be, as they say, out of my league.

~

There's no such thing as the perfect time or the best way to tell loved ones about your poetic inclinations. You need to muster up every ounce of courage in your being and just say it: *I'm a poet*. You could say 'I write poetry', but there's something non-committal about that phrasing, like you only dabble now and then and would prefer not to attach labels to your preferences. Prepare yourself for a full spectrum of emotional reactions, from 'You're still the same person to me' to 'I can't be friends with a poet'. And it's true—some people do think poets lead immoral lifestyles, and that enjambment is the slippery slope to the decay of civilisation. The night I finally told my parents, I had returned home from a book launch, tears streaming down my face, my body attempting to reject the awful chardonnay I'd been drinking all night. At the launch, I was overcome with a sudden need to come clean, no longer willing to hide my drafts in shoeboxes under my bed or a labyrinthine folder structure on our shared family computer that my brother later told me wasn't as effective as I thought it was. Perhaps it was the emotionally charged poem the poet had read about her relationship with her parents, or maybe I just can't process white wine like I used to. Whatever the catalyst, it all came out: the creative writing workshop I'd secretly taken at university; the poems I'd published in a handful of journals; and the poet who had urged me to tell them everything. My mother sobbed, her body slumped over our dining table. 'What will other people think? Our son—a poet! You won't be able to make a living!'. My father kept his distance, not knowing what to say or do. I can't imagine he's personally known any poets in his lifetime, nor had friends whose children turned out to be poets.

~

I'm ready to settle down with another poet, one who is also over getting drunk at readings and launches, and waking up next to a different stranger every morning during Writers Week. I see poet couples sharing copies of *The World Doesn't End* on park benches and I think to myself: that's what I want. Someone who helps me with my titles and tells me when I have too much white space showing, a voice of reason who lets me know when what I've written has gone too far, or hasn't gone far enough. Someone who makes me want to be a better poet—who won't be jealous that none of these poems are about them.

Selfie with landscape

Let's unpick what you think you know
about me—what I've revealed, what I've left
at the door of my favourite wolf, to force
eye contact the next time we pass
in the street. These stories all had emergency exits,
just like the rules adhered to by poets and liars
that we've never thought to record
for consistency's sake. Sometimes
I look at my face in a mirror and
all I see is a bruised blanket of dusk settling
on an increasingly unfamiliar terrain. I'm a man
who lets trouble back into his life
even though I have razed every highway
to and from that particular story. I'm both
a short breath and an age expanding into
minutes and days to be recycled as fact
by other writers in 100 years. Will they give
weight to my failed desires? Tell them I am
no vessel for their designs—sticky nights
forged into a vigil. Here's a true story:
I cut my wolf out of my night scenes
with a dull knife. He did not protest, and
therein lies the pathos. Here's a status update:
I cut my nails and now I can't scratch at the dust
caking over my eyes. I'll take a picture and
show the world what I'm too scared to keep
private. I just want them to like what I'm not.

MASC

Another poet's book is launched into the world
as being 'masculine'—   Coltrane, oil change, accidentally
                                  brushing a breast.

This book—   Madonna, selfies, inability
                                  to grow a beard.

                        ~

I launch myself   into dating apps
                 as a type*—geek, guy
                             next door, jock (ha!).

I have a type, but   I am not that type

so when my eye is caught
I know I'm looking
for edges on a white wall
like placing my optimism
                    into the path of oncoming traffic.

And still I wish, and still I play,
handicapped for not being
born with a full set of the desired teeth.

But
I am very many
                and I have a thirst for multiplication.

---

* *types—seen/unseen*   a brief history of the Asian male as an object of sexual desire
                         white bread in a multi-grain world
                         a MASC4MASC bull in a china shop
                         closeted daddies in offices ready to see their 1.30pm fuckbois
                         a silver lining for every dead faggot
                         double agents in gay bar restrooms
                         men who Frankenstein their own white saviour

This house

'No stranger's feet will enter me'.
— Kate Bush

1. This house is full of my mess

I had my paths and floor plans set, but
somewhere in the midst of someone else's
narrative, parts of me left the same room
through separate doors. No obvious
pinpoints, not in this subplot. Endured but
not endorsed; a sledgehammer to drywall.
The plaster flecks like damaged snow. This is
not my life anymore. This is not engagement.
Glass speaks of never seeing, as both sides, and
wood is burdened by the whims of time.
What to do now with those career prospects
and the heaving expectation of creative
endeavour? Use hunger as drive; nothing
starves me more than when ambition sings.

2. This house is full of mistakes

I think of my childhood home, stripped
of its internal organs and rendered lame.
On the day of separation, I visit its shell form
and take memories from each room before
realising this is my first time alone in
the house. To be present amid the curses
of a house scorned, that is a mourner's meal.
It dawns on me that I have been writing
about the wrong houses my entire life.

Mismatched wallpaper, nonsensical
colour schemes. Like rabbits is to hats
as secrets is to closets, I'll build
a new house and call it antiquity, plans
and growth spurts set in door jambs.

3. This house is full of madness

A life traversed without seasoning—
that is The Fear that locks me. Insulation
kept my house dry and muffled the sound
of doubt swimming through the walls
but now any talk of ambition paralyses
me. If—or when—noise control arrive
to confiscate these thoughts, I must decide
what to hide and what to show, always
conscious of what others may perceive
to be too much information even though
I will never know enough about *them*
to wield as insight. Every shadow cast
in this house is heavier now and the slack
doors have mastered the art of talking back.

4. This house is full of fight

Perhaps my parents will attend to my poems
and be taken aback by the presence of a certain
unnamed male, one who has found a place
to read and sleep in the best-lit room. This man
and I have shared more than each other's time.
He has a name (he'll always have a name) but
for now I leave him unidentified, a stand-in
for every boy lusted after from the first blush

of danger: the flawed; the taken; the straight boy
crushes; and the vindictive—each one furniture
in an unfamiliar house carelessly stashed away
in corners, conclusion-less. But with him there
was follow-through—safe passage between
rooms previously unexplored. A vivid dream.

Summer nights with knife fights

This is where you look up from your screens
to watch me   thrashing around
in a dream sequence—

                                  Tell me more, tell me more.

the night air slick with teenage grease
we pair off, disappearing
into friends' parents' rooms   garden sheds
under piers and bleachers
in station wagons with seats down/windows up
in darkened cinemas
while make-believe lovers make-believe kiss
in musical numbers   cleverly cut
to hide the outcasts pining
for their share of bloodlust.

                                  Tell me more, tell me more.

Are you the wolf?   *Yes.*
Are you the rose?   *Yes.*
Are you the sound of two bodies
turning into sand in hyperlapse?   *YES!*

I bet you say that to all the boys!

Danny glares at me from across
the gymnasium   with its stink
of youth and plastic cheer, grabs
his perky bulge and mouths
something homophobic. All the boys know
and that really turns me on. I can't help
but break   into song
as their fists meet my skin.

Tell me more, tell me more.

Meanwhile, Sandy
               and the ladies
hold a ritual cleansing to rid themselves
of their dipshit boyfriends.
               At midnight,
a wolf appears in the backyard, his huff
and his puff drawing them into
a breaking news story.
               And the world
will say they were asking for it.

Was it love at first fight?

Which part do you want to sing?
Really, *really* want to sing?

Would you ever let on
that you act like Danny
but would rather play Sandy?

―――――――――――――――――――――――――――――――――――

A hungrier wolf wouldn't know
what to do with a boy like me

a boy who joined a gang
to celebrate toxic masculinity
through the medium of musical theatre

a boy set to self-destruct
when his summer comes back to haunt him
with an Australian accent

a boy trading power ballads for masks
that don't quite conceal
the crack in his eyes.

Did you get very far?

―――――――――――――――――――――――――――――――――――

Love at first sight is your prerogative
when you're the world's
oldest teenagers—
          don't ever
let a casting agent tell you otherwise.

Pink lemonade, salty jokes and
knowing when to pull out
a call-and-response chorus
are all you need to pass for seventeen.
The audience will fill in the blanks
because that's what they think they're best at.

I'd ask you to dance again   caught under
taffeta and mirror-ball romance, but the boys
are heading out to race   and there's a chance
someone might die.

Isn't that why life is worth living? That you'll be
in the right place at the right time to witness
a teenage boy perishing in an act of bravado
after declaring his love for his best friend?

Because this doomed boy is just a body, after all.

And bodies can't help but be broken.

And the broken are meant to be sung about.

And the songs are meant to cut us.

I want wolf.
I need wolf.
But there ain't no way
I'm ever gonna wolf you . . .

The boy didn't die, and his friend will never love him.
We sing, regardless—it would be awkward not to.

The dashboard lights frame our faces
while our makeup cracks into life.
                              Stillness—
fake greenery—stunt emotions. A scared
teenage voice lifts from the back seat
and asks whether it's time
to switch sides.
                    Everybody knows
the end means boxing away your costumes
for the inevitable reunion, and everybody grows
into a thicker skin until then. It's a matter
of patience before we all move on
through the world to towns and cities
where wolves are more readily available
to take us dancing.
                    And these wolves
don't discriminate—boys, girls, other—
they are all suited to dressing their nights.

And   oh   oh   *OH!*

Those   summer   knife   FIGHTS!

CHRIS TSE AS DELETED SCENE:
The test audience said I didn't have the right look
to play a New Zealander   even though I
'sound   like   a   native   speaker'
so I got cut   out
and tucked away in DVD bonus feature hell.
I can sound like a dead bell in a hurricane too
or a confronting newspaper cartoon
or talkback radio hold music
or an episode of *Girls* that fails the Bechdel test
or hate crimes covered up as death by misadventure.

CHRIS TSE AS ASIAN HITMAN #1:
(non-speaking part)

QUESTION FROM THE AUDIENCE #1:
When I was a young girl growing up in 1960s Petone there were Chinese
kids at my school. Good grief—did their lunches smell! And when they
talk it's all *yabba yabba yabba*. I only ever made fun of them behind
their backs, and I walked to school with one whose family lived on my
street, so I couldn't possibly be racist. Look, there's nothing wrong with
the ones who have been here for generations. It's the new ones coming
here, buying our houses, and taking our jobs, and not making the effort
to understand our culture. I guess what I'm asking is—are you *really* a
third-generation Chinese New Zealander?

CHRIS TSE AS CHRIS TSE:
No, I just play one on TV.

QUESTION FROM THE AUDIENCE #2:
My question is in two parts. Aren't you being racist yourself by calling me
a racist? And what will you write about when you run out of otherness?

CHRIS TSE AS CHRIS TSE:
If by otherness
you really mean that rock in your fist
you really mean instructions for DIY walls
you really mean burning crosses
                            then
lest we forget whoever invented the faggot
say a little prayer for politicians who play
                    the Yellow Peril card
and raise your glass to the anonymous
                who haunt comments sections.

You see   although
            my oceans deep know no light and
                my sky is forever CinemaScope

        I have nowhere to hide.

        I know I have to trust my own body and voice
        like an understudy waits for that call to step up
                        and feel those eyes on him
        and know that they're all thinking

You are good, you belong
  on that stage, but you are not who we paid to see, you are not
            the one we were promised.

                My friends—I can be
            anything you don't want.

The compulsive liar's autobiography

He was born in a cave that you won't find on a map, where whales
sew their songs into stretches of beach and the tide unpicks their work.

~~My first word was 'truth'.~~

At eleven, he tap-danced the length of the country. The media branded
his backstory 'unauthorised to the edge of belief'. (Calls not returned.)

~~I staged the moon landing in my garage.~~

During the war, he murdered a one-eyed man whose name no one
remembers, though it's always on the tips of tongues, ready to leap.

~~I was New Zealand's first openly bisexual violinist.~~

He chanted daily into a charmed mirror—*I will be loved, I will be loved.*
The mirror looked back at him and could never believe what it saw.

~~I had three wives and one husband.~~

He fathered twenty children over eight industrious years. When asked
whether he knew any of their names, he started naming things in the room.

~~I know my first name is Steven.~~

He was questioned by police re: an incident at the zoo (animals broke in and
vandalised an enclosure). The evidence was allegedly destroyed in a fire.

~~I sold the cure for cancer to an African tribe.~~

The royalties from a sample in a hip-hop track funded a life-long passion
project: a musical about the disappearance of Lionel from *Shortland Street*.

I invented water.

He died in the arms of his lover, a man raised by wolves and fluent
in equations, the sort tipped to break through to the mainstream.

My cryogenically frozen body is hidden somewhere in Lower Hutt.

Pay no attention to that man behind the curtain!

Dare I dream of fame
yet live my life among
cardboard crowds?
                              This stands
to be examined—perhaps even
crushed—but I can't help myself
for wanting to appropriate the air
in a balloon or the colour of a baby's
flushed cheek for cheap
entertainment.
                        I want their ears
to want, but they can keep
their questions to themselves.
                        They treat my songs
with spotlights but deny them
curtains to hide behind.
                                Such songs
are tailored for weaker knees.

What do you hear now?

                The wheels of a tornado.
                        The strings of a storm.

                To veil, to veil—to no avail.

I've got enough to reveal
between my bars without them
                bringing an avalanche
                        to swallow my song.

Thunder's soul clap

I am turning into a weather system. With slow tongue
and an outlook for disaster, I am clouds conversing
with each other and lightning-strike spectacle.
                                    Nights are mild,
but it's the mornings that are hardest to get through, no thanks
to the smell of rain like cologne lingering long after a parting—
the cruellest of consolation prizes.
                                    We speak of thunder rolling
as if it were a body tumbling down a hill, across canvas plains,
unstoppable, gathering occasion as it passes through
small town after small town.
                                    On the news, they will gesture
at a map that isn't there and forecast its route—transforming,
rolling out—with no intent or motivation, with no resolve.
Once, I misread a news article, scanning the words
'rolling eyewitness account' as 'eye-rolling witness account'.
                                    We can be so cynical.
We can shake fists at the weather, blame the rain
for our bad days and build a case against snow.
                                    No system
will settle into a season without a tested reason. If I turn
to thunder, bury me in a valley far from where the lost
men dress up their wandering as songs. (These are the songs
we shouldn't trust to keep our feet dry.) Listen for my ache
on nights spent waiting for a sign.

I.R.L.

In real life
you are ageing at the rate of a short-lived sitcom

and the only kind of loneliness worth laughing about
is throwing out half a frozen meal for two

because leftovers
are never funnier the next day.

In real life
there is no such thing as a gritty reboot—it's just

fucking gritty all the time, mate
because your best-laid plans are always someone else's

chance to crash a car into the crowd at a
men's rights charity concert.

In real life
the nice guys pull out of the race

when their tyres are slashed or they turn back
because they think they left the iron on

and no one adheres to sports film clichés anyway—
we're all selfish and we want that trophy.

In real life
you'll never make it out of your homophobic small town

alive, so your left hand begs for water
while your right hand swings an axe

your left foot drags a church bell
while your right foot taps—S.O.S., S.O.S., S.O.S.

The saddest song in the world

1.

I can fit the saddest song in the world in my carry-on.
I can fit the saddest song in the world in my right-side brain.

But I can't fit it in my lungs or hold on to it with confidence
when underwater.   And I can't fit the saddest song

on one side of a 90-minute cassette tape without
an uncomfortable interlude cutting into its breath.

There is only so much space I can allocate to the saddest
song in the world;   the weight is unbearable.

2.

The saddest song in the world is the boy you kissed as a dare.
The saddest song in the world is a fist without purpose.

But the saddest song is not the worst day of your life
and it has never had its heart broken by the same man twice.

The saddest song in the world would never lose its keys
behind the couch or leave drowned teabags in the sink.

The saddest song in the world will treat you to a meal at
a fancy restaurant: twelve verses with matching wines.

When we sing our hope to pieces, the saddest song in the world
is there to provide notes.   It is honest, but constructive.

Every night the world shakes as the saddest song adds another
verse to its menu   then swallows the moon.

3.

Everybody knows the saddest song in the world. They loop
it in delivery rooms and maternity wards as Baby's First Song.

The saddest song in the world has no title, no lyrics, no melody,
no fixed abode: it floats between throats that harbour it

for those moments when we are in need of a voice
of reason   a song to frame the fog and light.

I have heard the saddest song in the world at night clubs.
I have heard the saddest song in the world at funerals.

I have heard the saddest song in the world during the credits
of films about forgotten artists and journeys into outer space.

The saddest song in the world is always ready
for its entrance, never once missing a cue.

4.

Once, a lover exhaled my name in ecstasy and transformed it
into the saddest song in the world   all bolting nerves

and tender skin   pulling at the roar of the avalanche
in me.   By morning, his name had taken another form

one freed from the haze of giddy crush   though it still rings in me
a stubborn joy.   The room in which we sung each other's names

is now an altar with no idol.   Likewise, when I was once lost
in the company of foreign tongues   every new word shared

to describe the sorrow of joy   shook me like the saddest song
in the world.   A list of first loves.   An index of loss.

The saddest song in the world was kind enough to pull me back
into comfort   its reassurances a cool blade of sound.

5.

Instruments and samples heard on the saddest song in the world:

My first guitar
Footsteps (snow)
String quartet in the rain
The last line of every romantic movie
Accordion with punctured lung
Tenor horn with stage fright
A dying horse's final wish
Footsteps (broken glass)
Baby's last word
His name
Movies about dying pets
A supercut of old men sobbing
Books burning in a town square
Lightning striking a country house
A single father scraping burnt toast
Dorothy letting go of Oz
A glimpse of a parallel
The last remaining pair of reading glasses (smashed)
Roy Orbison's 'Crying' | Rebekah Del Rio's 'Llorando'
Imagined duet between a grandfather and his grandson
An ex-lover sleeping in the next room
A prom queen's address to her people
'For sale: baby shoes, never worn'.

6.

Don't forget that sometimes people leave, that lines of
connection will be drowned by seas of noise. We hover

hands above stovetops to test for heat, but what can we do to
warn ourselves of impending absence? Don't forget to share

your sadness, in parcels sent from the mainland, your blacks and
blues in search of the spectrum. There are consequences to consider

when you share the saddest song in the world with desperate
people. Some will take its words and stretch them towards

new meanings, beyond their humble origins. It must mean
this, or it must mean *that*. But the song snaps back into place

like a rubber band, a muscle trained to withstand the momentum
of loss. They set houses on fire to entice the saddest song

back into their nights. The fires are colourless, lacking in rhythm
and harmony. They keep eating themselves before dawn.

7.

You wonder how one song can do so much with the same
number of hours in each day open to the rest of us. One minute

the song is spat from the windows of a passing car, the next
it's the ringtone of the teenage girl next to you on the bus.

Hours later you shuffle home from work and catch
the saddest song being interviewed on TV, still bright and ready,

about the latest political scandal. This productivity makes
no sense to you. In fact, it downright stings you in your palms.

Hang the cross out to dry. Time is a side worth fighting for,
to gather your children in an empty room and teach them

the meaning of patience. Let the saddest song pull the oxygen
from the room, just enough to let you slip unknowingly into

the next day. When the time comes, let me pull you from
the orchestra pit, your body waxing itself into a new tune.

I will usher you to where the saddest song will be waiting
for you—yes, *you*—with a mouth eager to drink your hum.

8.

I met a woman who claimed to have been married to
the saddest song in the world.   She showed me

a discoloured photo of their wedding day and pulled her dress
out of a box marked 'Misc'.   Nobody came to the wedding

except for the woman's neighbour and a passer-by
who successfully negotiated an appearance fee.

The saddest song stayed silent during the ceremony
keeping its reservations to itself yet again

just like all its other weddings.   Yes, this was not the first time
the saddest song in the world had been married.   Nobody ever

accuses the saddest song in the world of being a con artist or
polygamist.   It is merely giving people the chance to experience

its company for themselves with no influence from outside noise.
The saddest song in the world just wants to know you're happy.

Slice the saddest song in half and the rings you see won't give you
its age: each ring is another betrothal to another anxious soul,

each one more complicated than the last.   The saddest song
in the world spends half its annual income on spousal support.

Times are tough: radio is fickle and MTV no longer plays music.
The saddest song in the world needs a new distribution model.

9.

When the saddest song in the world dies there will be no obituary
or funeral.   There will be no opportunistic tribute albums or

documentaries, and musicians will not issue sappy statements
recalling how the saddest song influenced their own work.

You will know the second it has happened. Perhaps you'll be
in your car listening to an argument on talkback radio

or in your backyard collecting washing from the line.
It will be a *where were you when it happened?* moment,

only no one will actually know what it is that has happened.
The air will appear thinner for the briefest of seconds

and your neighbour's dog might start snapping at an invisible guest.
The lifetime of loss you carry draped over your shoulders

will take its cue to fall away.   You will make out
for the first time   the sound of birds diving through clouds

as the saddest song in the world glides into its fade out.
The saddest song in the world has left the building.

Present tension

Winter claims your shoulders first. Your neck tenses.
You side-step a dead hedgehog that keeps getting moved
from pavement to gutter and back again, like the world's
simplest but least sanitary chess game. Back and forth
until someone concedes, or when the corpse falls apart.
There's no strength in numbers when the number is one.
Waiting for a bus at this time of the year is like cycling
through the stages of grief, and there's always a cup of tea
at the end of it. You keep telling yourself: *Remember,*
there was light yesterday, and sound too. The guy next to you
mumbles something about a sandy beach, or maybe
it's a sandy bitch. Your focus cracks in this cold.
The overhead wires hum. The cellphone orchestra stabs.
Your body has never embraced the sounds of the present.
Maybe you'll start to make an effort when you separate
necessity from decency. Of course, no one cares which
way you jump. Throw your voice to frame your fingers.
Throw your frame around the moon. Look back from
that lock and ask our world to be reasonable. Ants and
speckles. Toe-dips and smudges. Why bother undoing
when time comes back around to bite you in the arse?

New mythology

Our sight lines are parallel to the slip of water
that scores where we end

and all our grand gestures accumulate and wave
goodbye. When the wind buffets

against our faces, it produces a Larsen effect.
Through this

we can measure the way melody enters then leaves
a body, like an old friend

lost to old games, stepping back over the line
to embrace you. Picture

the beauty of the motorway at night, that lullaby
stretch, channels

of humming grey gliding into the wild possibilities
of each morning.

Here is your exit; here are your shadow lands.
Place yourself.

When a city is a myth, the future is so ready
to betray it with an unstable outlook.

There is no faith in a stolen place; the storytellers
have made that much true.

I want things that won't make me happy

I want neon; I want that snap in my veins. I want
showtime lights sweeping me into deep, relentless
fever.   Give me calamity.   Give me soul
to get me through the final gate. I chose disco
and look where it got me—dancing
with a smile I cannot sell.
It's like   every time I go
out clubbing and flirting
I come home with another skeleton to bury.
Sometimes I resort to using silence as means
to cut him   loose; an easy exit
from a poorly lit party   but not before
          many, many kisses from
                    many, many men.
A better version of the latest model
          to lick the curve of his bicep as it winks at me
                    for the world to retweet my pain.

Lupine

When I was a young wolf undergoing transformation
that trickster moon, so rich with gravitational pull,
drew the buried beast out of me. Stalking the streets
with my sharpened howls seeking out the night
I set my sights on warm hearts whose keepers did not
believe in my kind or in fear. Something in their delusion
dragged at my thirst, which had no trouble finding
its way into their homes and shelters. I showed them fear.
Such were my nights for years as a fallow soul; I shed my
goatskin and terrorised. I licked their wounds with glee
until one chanced night the moon refused my skin.
The beast did not come. Confused and rejected, I ran
until I dipped headfirst into a solemn silver lake not knowing
whether I was unravelling in a spent dream or simply drowning.

I made it through the wilderness

He could tell I was a desperate teenage boy, ready for him to be
my first. It was a weekday afternoon, and instead of unpacking

Citizen Kane with classmates I found myself a player in that great cliché:
two strangers in a toilet stall. Just him and me: hands given

places to grope, lips given reasons to part. Then, when he suggested
we take things further, I followed him to a secluded spot

deep in the cemetery, the chattering headstones still visible through
the trees. Just him and me: his eyes too welcoming, too eager

to take me into his gaze. As I pulled myself into him, I thought: this is
my life from now on, a parade of nameless encounters, unprepared

for how alone I could feel when entangled with another. Why did I
mark an otherwise unremarkable day with skin on skin and

a tasteless man? Because my best friend had beaten me to it with ease
many years ago and had called after the event to give me the details.

Because I needed to know whether what they said about me was true.
'How can this be your first time?' the First Man asked. Later, picking

dead leaves from my hair and lying about my absence to my friends,
I knew exactly how: I had learned to turn my body into my greatest

disguise. I could be anyone and every man could be my first time
if I threw my voice just so—just me, slipping out of *mise-en-scène*.

Fast track

Boys—you are not immortals   not placed once upon
        a line
             from the gods   nor traced back
             from a point
                  less than zero.

There is no greatness for you to claim
           when the world is filled with boys
                  like you.

Boys—you are not invincible
          especially when your games become
               bloodsports for others
             with money on your pain.

Your bravado is the evening news   on repeat
        swaying the hours
             until the world finds a
               new outrage.

Boys—you fight only yourselves
      when negotiating with flags
          that cut out the chase—

BE MASC   NO FEMMES
BE HUNG   NO ASIANS
BE FIT   NO FATTIES
BE STRAIGHT-ACTING   NO QUEENS

Boys—you will find love
          but love no man until he is ripe
          in the head

his colours bright
in all casts.

Do not love him   until he is ready to follow you
with shared words
      and you both accept
      that there is no fast track
          to halls of fame.

Time is wasted when you settle
    for a man   who, in his own denials, inflicts
        a colourless wound. That seam
   you ignore is where
      disease gets in
    and turns your body against you.

   One bad thought
   changes everything.

Boys—you will lose.
      We will all lose.
      Ice caps melt. Extinction erases.
      The Earth will loose itself
        from its alphabets.

Every word
    and story will fall into space
        after the world's amnesia
      stirs it into slumber.

    There will be nothing left
        to spread your glories.

Boys—you will die.

Desire

That pinpoint year I trawled through cyberspace
collecting covers of Springsteen's 'I'm on Fire'.

~

All to impress a boy   just out of reach
a kind of infatuation marked   by slow burn and humming.

~

Some howl like tortured lovers   others reclaim
the valley between sex and death as their own kingdom.

~

Tipped upside down you tore the sky
with your silver tongue   talked me into running with you.

~

Here comes the train again
spitting   shuffling   driverless.

Boy meets wolf

He is my wolf—he with the teeth
that come out at night

and a hand that shows me where
to claim his edges.

I must not wreck my body
over his

in reaching for what lies beyond
this single night.

Consider starts that never slip
past *GO*

and blunt endings thrown before
a child can grow.

My drunken nerves, my entire day—
like a space bar brings me

ocean upon ocean of
in-between—at a time

when I'm trying to hum
a very particular note

but hit everything else either side
of the harmony.

All calm voices suggest I should
throw him back into the wild

into thorns nestled between
a dream and escape.

I spy my wolf from the cliff
when he leaves

to gather food. This wolf has a
sweet tooth; it leads

him to fast-moving rivers beyond
the borders we agreed.

I use the day to sharpen my claws
ready for sparring

ready to let this wolf back in
to where he doesn't belong.

Choose your own adventure

If attraction, say yes
If rejection, start again

If film, turn to common tastes
If cocktails, turn to unknown pleasures

If house party of friend-of-friend,
       bring your own backstory

If uncomfortable silence,
       no exit until first light

If destiny, prepare for cruelty
If cameo-turned-plot-twist, say you saw it coming

If celebratory, find gold dust in your pockets
       twelve hours after the fact

If causal, link left to right
       shoulder to shoulder, carry on

       let the cartilage crunch
       (it draws upon transition

       from your teenage fumbling
       to your daring twenties)

If new and unknown, do not shrink into yourself
If dissociative, cut your losses

If temporary, find the time
       and accept that pain is on its way

       allow yourself to see it coming
       at least three turns before the end

A star like no other

If a star—like a bare bone cleaned of everything pink—took his place,
then perhaps that would swing me. I would fail, once again, to be metal.

~

'That is sunlight peeking through your seams', said the moon.
'That is too much muscle for such a simple act of raising lanterns
and holding him close'.

                              So I dropped
my arms, resumed stasis. As it turns out, that
is too much sky for a single star to bear.

~

Stars with sparrow tattoos. Stars with Russian memoirs.

The headlines fall off the pages, go swimming
in my morning coffee.

Stars in the arch of an eyebrow. Stars twitching under blankets.

~

I see stars, and I have written him into mine.
I am still brushing his ashes from my sheets.

Distance getting close

Distance begins
with knowing what is closest to you.

~

It's the release of the dampers
at 2.38 of 'Tear in Your Hand'.

In that moment, you hear the band exhale
in unison

but it's really just an echo
trapped in the piano

                all the time
in the world catching up with itself.

Time to wave goodbye now.
Time to tear throats out

to prick the sky and let
whatever's behind the blue   piss out.

~

The cruellest measures:
a lover's ballad set to the speed of rain

a sustained note choked by nerves
a foot tapping out of time with the rest of the band.

~

The human body stores an unspecified amount
of distance, yet watch how it struggles to reach out

to the points it knows are there. The fires
on the horizon chatter with full lungs.

Instead of simply letting the rain tear down
we run as fast as we can with full buckets.

~

The first night with someone new
always challenges what you're accustomed to:

how to fit your arm under his shoulder
or whether you should turn

to face each other. Then you begin
to panic about the gap

between your breaths.   With your
contacts out

you can only just make out
his lips. Are his eyes closed or open?

You inch closer. You pull him in.
You borrow air from his lungs

and let yourself take flight.
It's not just the inches you struggle

to close; it's the 3.1059m²
of bed   you flounder in

with your personal histories.
Past escapades aren't to be

mentioned, only shut
behind the eyes.

This is what it means to close distance,
to allow yourself to follow a masked man

down a dark alley with your heart
turning   in his hands.

Release

Not before I stir you
from your sleep, and ask whether
this is the last time I'll see you
before you hop that plane
for Sydney. We'll hold
each other, cheek to cheek,
when we both hear
the answer.

Not before you slip
on your trousers, hunt for your wallet
and down a glass of water.
The city slept in your eyes
last night, traces of its troubles
linger in your morning sigh.
You'll be groggy but gorgeous,
your unkempt beard diligently framing
the gentle smile of a boy borrowed
from the stars. You make it so hard,
you know—this letting go.

But not before we embrace, kiss
deeply in my bedroom, the kitchen,
and twice on the street outside
my apartment building.
          (Before you, I had neither
          the chance nor the courage to kiss a guy
          in public. In the Botanic Gardens
          just weeks earlier, metres
          from an audience,
          you asked, *Can I steal a kiss*
          or are you being spied on?

I told you I didn't care
who might be watching.)
On this particular morning
the construction site across the road
will be all steel and no music.
The sky will mock us with its clarity.

And not before a day
of blank expressions, stumbling
through the mediocrity
of PowerPoint and strategic objectives,
returning home to
duvet, sheets and pillows
hastily abandoned
and finally finding the time
to cry.

Not before I gather up
and wash the bedding.
But not the pillow cases—
they'll still hold your scent
for a few hours more. Later that night
I will pull the pillows close
and cry again, embarrassed
at my reaction to the expanse
of bed left to me.
The heart is heaviest
when it is empty
when a lover has removed himself
from every fold and corner.

And not before I lose half a day
rewriting an email
a dozen times over before trashing it,
then waiting for a text or a call

from you to say you've changed
your mind—you'll stay
in this faraway city of mine
with your unnecessary hiking boots.
I'll put aside my aversion to camping
and together we could find
a time and place for them.

But my city isn't chaotic enough for you
and I will always hate dirt and camping.
There are adventures for you to collect
on other full-moon nights and you have
your life to write
                elsewhere.

The books by my bed
will still tell me beautiful lies and
every passing song will fill my head
with the empty spaces of you—
even the dance songs (especially
the dance songs).

              And then
there is the song you have taken
from me, replaced with poems
that mean nothing to anyone else.
I try to sing every syllable
of your name, to fill the room once again
with what was always temporary.
But yours is a name
I cannot release. To do so would
fool me into thinking
you're still within reach.

Astronaut

In his dreams
             the mouth of night
is mute   from a year of troubled star-gazing

terrified and unwilling   to explain
the idea of   tomorrow
        to a boy   averse to propulsion.

        ~

No news from the control centre
regarding signs of new life. (The adoring astronomer
                    disarmed by scientific intent.)

This is the twenty-first century: surely we have
the technology to instil hope   or at the very least
        encourage us to believe in the *idea* of hope.

        ~

He holds his breath   and thinks dangerous
thoughts   of lightning   shooting skywards
        from his eyes.

Each blunt day brings   another reason to pray
        or hours spent hanging on
stars that never return   his attention.

        ~

Gravity, orbits:
                    unforgiving attraction
to the things that draw us near but never reach out.

Still no news.   Still no signs.
                These slow days
            draw out   with marbled static.

The opposite of music

(*The day after*) Distance and silence: the only two things I find in the space he left.

~

(*Idea*) A one-man flash mob in Times Square, but no one's watching.

~

(*Analogy*) I buried his body in Central Park—next to the tree where he and I first kissed—because I couldn't afford a cemetery plot.

~

(*We talked about the future*) Sunlight eating shadow off the face of Mount Everest—big scoops of powdered sugar on anxious crackers.

~

(*Cautionary tale*) Cinderella always fucks up with daylight savings.

~

(*I found you again*) A troupe of drag queens are covering the Bee Gees' 'Tragedy', only they have changed the title to 'Travesty'. You can tell which of them can't shake the original.

~

(*Unlikely story*) It's true—I am guilty of disco, and every afterthought of me will be that go-to song during '70s-themed telethons.

~

(*Radio silence*) As I have taken to despair with gusto, so have you to disappearing acts. These winter nights are just the right length for such crafts.

~

(*Feel-good movie of the year*) The satellites we sent to space will never find their way home. Instead, they'll be adopted by couples who could never have children of their own. Their homes always smell of soup.

~

(*Six months*) Thought bubbles—speech rubble—staring into your bathroom mirror and asking your reflection, 'Am I gym toned yet?'.

~

(*He—she—we*) When she sings her newborn to sleep the melody she chooses is old paint tossed from a moving vehicle at a refugee family. Red stains the pavement and raves throughout a sticky summer.

~

(*Thank you to the Academy*) Not the boy in the song crying at the disco; not the girl with two fake deaths to her name.

~

(*Reminders*) The ex-lovers as an iPod on shuffle; a road trip playlist; a rent-a-rapper remix; another 'Hallelujah' cover; a mondegreen.

~

(*A year later*) When I Google your name, you are displaced as the top search result by an eyewitness of a school shooting in New Mexico. He looks nothing like you. You are so entrenched in my search history that there's no turning back.

MacGuffin

To say the briefcase is pertinent
is to ignore the man in
the speckled grey suit slouched
by the pay phone, moustache
ready to turn villain,
his concealed gun pressed squarely
against his ribcage. You can tell
he's a baddie because
he doesn't blink and looks straight
into the camera like he couldn't
give a fuck. To express
that the film did not commit
to the characters' intents is to
impose your own logic, tongue
lashing at the masses, not able to
turn their eyes to the dirty light
tainting the walls
of bathroom stalls
used for hook-ups and quick
fixes. There: the clinical *plink*
of syringes falling to the floor
and fluorescent tubes realising
illumination. At this point, we are
questioned about our own intent
as an audience of willing
accomplices. Our eyes dilate.
What will it take for us to stop
resorting to tradecraft
to pull each other into honest
dialogue? Some of us rely on
our gift of good timing; our days
are hung on it. The rest of us

second-guess The End. I never
walk out on films because
I hate to see a story go
unfinished. You are more
likely to walk, whereas I could
never leave you. But there's
the door, and I'm told the sky
is particularly bright tonight.
It only takes a little moonlight
to test your commitment
to a role.

Still—the boys

Perhaps you'd like to dance with this one
Perhaps you'll trace the lines of that one

                    Neither boy
has heard of Ani DiFranco

You suspect they were both born
                        well after *Dilate*

and the first electronic deaths
of neglected Tamagotchi

            little god complexes/little 8-bit screams

'It's a toy for girls', its makers said

Like how some boys are for girls
and the rest fall into beds with each other

without the right words to use the morning after
in rooms too small for silence

Boys you bang out on typewriters
Boys you regret leaving behind in backseats

Such desires and frustrations never expire
no matter how accustomed you are to salt

Still—the boys
they are waiting to dance   and sleep

and you have been open to rule-breaking
for so long   Perhaps, perhaps etc.

Notes for Taylor Swift, should she ever write a song about me

I look for men like I look for nouns, though
I have very little use for them once I find them.
I write out their names like blank cheques
and put my trust in their honesty. I revise
my lists until I have no time to action them.
Yes, they're meant to be an efficient exercise
in compartmentalisation, but there's always
something I've overlooked so I rip them up
and start again. Like they say—once more
with feeling! I lack the mechanics to say no,
but I do have the common sense to run away
from falling pianos. Some men I've loved
have lacked that initiative. I'm destined
to be a poster boy without a cause,
without a slogan. But you can at least
give me a chance, right? Make me a hit song
for the ages—the last great crossover ballad.

Sweetheartbreaker

The world ends on a Thursday. By oblivion
there is a new king—one with hands poised
over the waning body of a deer too slow
to outrun wolves. The new king carries the deer
across a frozen river. Its grave will be bottomless.
Accept the fact that you have no say in which skin
is shed or which tower casts the coldest shadow.
After this end—and before the next beginning—
you would've traded your pulp for an escapist fuck.
Is that how you should entertain yourself in the midst
of grief? A vulnerable man sacrificed and dignity
damned. These wolves expect a bloody hunt, not a
wounded lay. You offer your husk but they do not bite.
The harm's done—Friday is the new rest of your life.

Next year's colours

*When I take a picture of the city it disappears / It's only a
photograph—the city is gone / The places I go are never there
. . . / Nostalgia isn't what it used to be / I can only picture the
disappearing world when you touch me.*

— Sam Phillips

I always return home from holidays with more photos than I'll
ever need. Somehow it's worse when it's a city I've been to before—
as if subconsciously I'm correcting the photos I've taken on previous
visits, challenging the course of my experiences.

At some point, I'll sit down and decide how these photos might
tell the story of hours spent wandering unfamiliar streets for 'best
hidden secrets' and jostling against other tourists for the best view.
Every possible narrative is a disappearing act.

We open ourselves up to failure with everything we choose to hold
on to. Eventually, my own memory fails to remind me why I took a
particular shot or why I chose to turn a certain corner.

Every tourist takes more or less the same photographs—public
forgeries without a definitive original, ghostly trails of our desire
to stake our claim of a shared memory. And it is a shared memory—
think of the thousands of photos that you could possibly be in,
a background extra in someone else's holiday slideshow.

~

This is a photo of a building.

It meant something to me at the time.

This is a photo of the sky.

It meant something to me at the time.

This is a photo of a two strangers meeting.

It meant something to me at the time.

~

From steep skyward lines, from inverse reaction, from the moment light is caught and begins to fade—the colours show themselves out when they are no longer needed, when they are ready to fill in the next set of memories.

~

In New York City, I started thinking about next year's colours, like next year's black and next year's one-hit wonder—each colour recovered from a photograph or a hastily scrawled list in my notebook:

THE FIRST AND THE LAST
A BRAVE SOUL
A HAND TO HOLD
A SONG FOR ONE

Were these the things I wanted to be, or the things I wanted to find? How many chances do we get to look into the past before the paper wears thin or the names and dates begin to conspire against us?

~

I logged on to dating apps out of curiosity—the kicking-distance proximity of the nearest man a strange unit to me. Grid after grid of headless torsos and pseudonymous men—a crowdsourced Warhol for the selfie age— profile photos carefully shot, edited and filtered until these men had created a new cover story for themselves, the best version of whatever it was they wanted to disguise. These men were all so ready to dance, and I'm never dressed for a rave. Their words would bite like mosquitoes, drawing blood until I found a way to shake them off. The way they talked to me made it feel like my face or my desires weren't mine anymore. I could no longer lay claim to who I thought I wanted to be. With each blunt word they swiped at my features until I was someone they could do terrible things to. A grope. A slow dance. A quick handjob in a Starbucks restroom. The offers of kisses were the worst.

Where are you? they would ask.

I don't know—I'm new here—I can't see the sun from where I'm standing but I can hear water and a woman crying.

Where are you?

I don't know—It's my first time—I thought I was in New York—I thought I was here.

You're close. So close.

~

Water to water—quietly, blind with stars—tips of scrapers ascend this city that once bled dust and paper. The sky here is so stiff with white noise that we throw rhythm at it to dig out the weakness in its joints.

We pitch these buildings up around us and then spend our lives wondering where we are among them. We consider how we are all part of a plural, no matter where we might be standing. When we add sex and dislocation, that's when things get really interesting.

~

Should a photographer ever return to the spark of a memory?

Should a hook-up ever return to the scene of the crime?

~

Pick a day—any day. Now remember that day. Don't tell me. Just let it slip back and settle into where you store those 'Where were you when . . . ?' moments.

Magic fools the memory through misdirection—your eyes are always stuck on the one thing you shouldn't care about. That's how they get you. You study, you analyse, you search for meaning, but the real show is always happening just out of sight.

I watched the sunset swirl patterns in the Hudson, a watercolour stain rippling out into edgeless blur. A young woman next to me cried as she tore up a stack of photos—moments with her boyfriend (a magician) and once beloved city skylines that were too painful to hold on to now that he was forever linked to that day. She told me that she no longer believes in magic. She's spent so many years trying to convince people that magic is real, but now that the city is finding ways to celebrate its scars, it feels futile. *It's just not the New York I remember*, she sighed.

~

It can be just as hard to let go of a city as it is to let go of a man, especially when that man is miles of water and borderlines away. You may as well gift your heart to the next in line.

New York is the man with an opera tucked under his arm, like a newspaper or a small dog. The newspaper, if rolled tightly, can do impressive damage, whereas the dog bites and sneers with diamond teeth. The last time I saw New York he held my face and wouldn't let go. Even as my plane took off he held on, his feet running through the air just like a cartoon character. At 10,000 feet he finally loosened his grip. He fell to earth so quickly—didn't even make a sound as his body tore itself apart. A year's worth of newspapers splashing through the sky; that small dog finally shown who's boss.

~

On my last morning in New York, I had coffee with one more stranger. In graphic detail, but quietly so that the elderly couple in the adjacent booth couldn't hear, he told me all the depraved things we could have been doing to each other had either of us had a place to host (he'd checked out of his hotel room and my two travelling companions were still sleeping in ours). I could tell he had recounted this fantasy many times—perhaps even as a conquest boast among friends. I had no feedback for him, constructive or otherwise. When he was done, he took a photo of me on his phone and told me this would be the closest he'd ever get to New Zealand.

~

Next year's colours will be fashioned from whatever city I leave behind and the photographs I take home with me. They will be set to songs discovered on free CDs attached to glossy magazine covers. American actors will endorse them in Japanese television commercials they think no one will ever see. The memories—the fading ones—will have no say in the matter, not now that they have cut the art between us with a cheap and dirty blade.

I visit cities and in turn they visit me—in shadow lines scrawled in notebooks and photos gathering dust (literal and digital). On the topic of my own past, I am a teacher wielding a red pen, slipping in words I wish I'd known and laying proof for the years to come.

This is a photo of a photo of a building.

It meant something to me at the time.

This is a photo of a photo of the sky.

It meant something to me.

This is a photo of myself taking a photo of two strangers.

It meant something.

Spot the difference—Answers

The man to the left of the seesaw
      is missing his right hand.
The seesaw is now a canoe.
The canoe, carved from the rib
      of a mammoth, has docked
      between two national flags.
The striking, bearded gentleman
      in the foreground is you.
The smudge to the right of the scene
      is my missing right hand
      is my persistence.
The day is now night.
The summer is now an orchestration
      of clouds, sharking me all day.

Crying at the disco

The girls   I thought I loved
still follow me around—

        they are scare quotes
          in all subsequent drafts.

The boys   I watch dancing together
are so bright

      the walls begin to crack.

They are both sides
    of a record—a beauty

           and an anecdote.

Every time   I think about you
in loud places such as this

    I dance   until my heart breaks.

I can't see you when your eyes are closed.

      And I can't hear you over the rush

of bodies   exhausting themselves
breaking down   and breaking up.

    I need you

like a whisper needs a shout
    like a sad song needs a gentle cold ending.

Ends, actually

You surprise yourself
                by being able to laugh so soon after.

It pulls the shades down behind your eyes
                and seals in that last glance and whisper.

Tenuous is the curve bearing
                the trauma delivered by arrows

that cry down and pierce your mask's
                slick ambition, too clever for shields,

but—oh, how sweet!—the one you least suspect
                kneels down to take off your dancing shoes.

Like a child driven by discovery,
                stars and planets in full view,

you'll store this as a touchstone
                for the times you'll need to shatter on demand.

You can have teeth if teeth will tear
                away the unnecessary wrapping

because if all that ends is an echo riding
                on an available light beam to the next pair of eyes

you may consider setting yourself on fire to know
                what it's like to be the source of a memory.

Spanner—A toast

To be the sun.
To be locked in the care
of glass.
          To show, then offer.
To know that love
is the most dangerous
sting yet to still give up an arm.
          To wake from machines
and know your hope will
never be yours alone.
To take to those machines
as an unexpected spanner.
          To fill a touch
          with a complete
          backstory.
To leave sugar
at my door to keep
you close. To crave

          but not seek.
To know the future and
avoid it. To accept that
after silk comes rain
from dark, honest clouds.
To lose a smile
at a storied game of chance.
To let the morning
sweep away
the last nine months.
To wrong no other
even when the line's
          gone dead.

To family and friendship.
To starts, to ends,
to towers
we go.

Wolf spirit—Fade out

There's a song you
cannot trust to
keep you bathed in
colour. It pounds

        like a '90s
        piano house
        track until your
        legs turn to smoke.

It fades into
shadow; it stops
smiling when you
enter a room.

        The last light falls
        from your face as
        the moon carves its
        way out of the

sky. This song is
the death of the
wolf—is the death
of days you thought

        you were both still
        singing—passing
        into wild youth,
        diminishing

from earshot. Just
be happy for
having danced with
the wolf, his clear

        solitaire eyes,
        his tracks in your
        history. Be
        brave—press repeat.

Notes and acknowledgements

Some of these poems first appeared in *Atlanta Review, Best New Zealand Poems, Cordite Poetry Review, Cyphers, Glitterwolf, Ika, JAAM, Mimicry, New Zealand Poetry Shelf, Poetry, Queen Mob's Tea House, Rejectamenta, Snorkel, The Spinoff, Sport, takahē,* and *Turbine.* Many thanks to the editors of these publications.

The other poet's book mentioned in 'MASC' is Bill Nelson's excellent *Memorandum of Understanding*.

The epigraph and section titles for 'This house' are from Kate Bush's song 'Get Out of My House'.

'Next year's colours' was originally commissioned by City Gallery Wellington and LitCrawl as a response to Fiona Pardington's 'Photograph' (2015). The epigraph is from Sam Phillips' song 'Taking Pictures'.

*

Thank you to Mum and Dad; Leight and Jo; Team Kylie + Carly (Francis Cooke, Louise Wallace and Gem Wilder); the team at Auckland University Press; Sarah Jane Barnett; Greg Simpson; Rajeev Mishra, Daniel Christie and Jeremy Veal; Kirsten Campbell; Rebecca McMillan; Claire Mabey and Andrew Laking; Andy Wong and Peter Agar; Hawthorn Lounge; and my family and friends, near and far.